ONE

30-Day Couple's Devotional

A Guide to Developing and Maintaining Oneness

David & Sylvia Banks

Scriptures taken from the following versions

ERV, ASV, and ESV – Public Domain

Scripture taken from the Holy Bible, MODERN KING
JAMES VERSION copyright© 1962 —1998 by Jay P.
Green, Sr. Used by permission of the copyright holder.

Printed in the United States of America

First Printing, May 2020

ISBN 978-0-578-69132-9

About David & Sylvia Banks

David Banks, Ph.D., is a certified relationship coach, and a certified professional coach with expertise in relationships, leadership development, motivation, and purpose discovery. Dr. Banks conducts training in the United States, India, Mexico, Pakistan, Australia, and Trinidad & Tobago. He and his bride Sylvia are founders of Noble Marriages, an organization to empower marriages to develop and maintain oneness. David & Sylvia Banks both have degrees in psychology.

Sylvia Banks is a teacher, mentor, and author. She is passionate about helping women excel in every area of their lives. She has developed and taught two courses: "Women of Excellence" and "Time for ORDER." She is the author of "The 7 Pillars of a Noble Woman". David and Sylvia authored a marriage book: "Draw Me Close." They reside in Chattanooga, TN, with their children, Benjamin, 27, Caleb, 23, and "Princess" Maiya Banks, 18.

Introduction

A Guide to Developing and Maintaining Oneness

Whether you are recently married, or you have been married for several years, creating a solid foundation is vital. The solid foundation is celebrated during the good times and a major anchor during tough times. Many marriages experience several stages that shape a couple's relationship.

We are familiar with the first stage, the honeymoon stage. This stage begins with the, "I do," vows. The groom kisses his new bride and they are officially introduced as Mr. & Mrs.

As they embark on their new life together their total focus is on each other. The honeymoon becomes a time of bonding, as they are separated from the demands and distractions of life.

It is every couple's dream to live in this oasis of love, however, "life" is patiently waiting for them to return.

As they settle into the rhythm of life, and begin to live "life," it slowly but surely begins to happen. Their attention turns to bills, finances, juggling schedules, work and eventually children. It happens subtly but before the newlywed couple realizes it, distance has crept into their relationship. They are not as close as they were when they said, "I do!"

When distance takes up residence in the couple's marriage, it invites uninvited "friends." These friends are *tension, assum* and possibly *distrust, lack of communication and taking each other for granted.* The couple is overwhelmed, and their relationship is overcrowded with all uninvited "friends." Sadly, most couples resort to two decisions.

The first decision couples choose is to tolerate their new additions and live a life of distance and disorder. The other option couples choose is divorce. Take heart! These are not the only options. There is another option; that option is called returning to *oneness.* That is the purpose of this **"30 Day Couple's Devotional."** A Guide to Developing and Maintaining Oneness. As a full disclaimer, the purpose of this couple's devotional is not designed to take you back to the altar of your wedding date and start over. This couple's devotional is created to start you where are now and move you towards *oneness* in marriage.

Here are the instructions of how to experience this couple's devotional

- Agree that you both desire to develop and maintain *oneness* in your marriage.

- Set aside 15 min to complete each devotional. Be intentional and consistent.

- You can complete each devotional daily for 30 days or on a weekly basis.

May each devotional inspire you to draw closer to experience long-lasting *oneness*.

Enjoy!

Day 1

Read

♦ *Psalms 127:1 "If it is not the LORD who builds a house, the builders are wasting their time. If it is not the LORD who watches over the city, the guards are wasting their time."*

Revelation

♦ Who needs to build your home?

♦ What is the result if the Lord doesn't build your home?

Responsibilities

♦ Are you both in agreement to allow the Lord to build your marriage and home?

Reverence (hold hands)

- Pray this prayer together: "Father, we realize that You need to be the builder of our marriage. We dedicate our lives and marriage to You. We commit to live a life that is pleasing to You. In Jesus' name, amen."

Date completed:

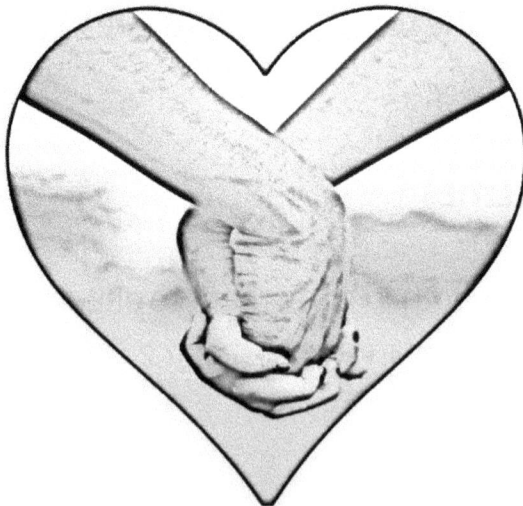

Day 2

Read

- *Genesis 2:24 "Therefore shall a man leave his father and his mother and shall cleave to his wife and they shall be one flesh."*

Revelation

- Whose responsibility is it to leave and cleave?
- What is the responsibility of the wife?

Responsibilities

- Take a picture of both of you holding hands, symbolizing you have become one.

REVERENCE (HOLD HANDS)

- Pray this prayer together: "Father, I pray that we will become one flesh in our marriage. Protect us from outside influences that try to attack our oneness. Empower us to stay intentional about developing and maintaining our oneness. In Jesus' name, amen."

DATE COMPLETED:

DAY 3

READ

- *Genesis 2:25 "And they were both naked, the man and his wife; and they were not ashamed."*

REVELATION

- Who was naked?

- Though they were naked, how did they feel?

- Are you comfortable being naked; physically, mentally, and emotionally?

RESPONSIBILITIES

- Share with each other your deepest dream in life.

Reverence (hold hands)

♦ Pray this prayer together: "Father, I pray that we will become totally transparent and vulnerable in our marriage without feeling ashamed. Give us the strength if we have violated each other's trust. Allow us to get to a point where we can be totally open with each other in every area of our relationship. In Jesus' name, amen."

Date completed:

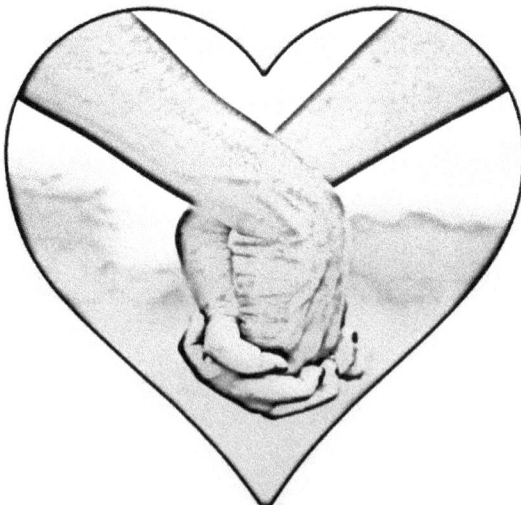

Day 4

Read

- *Genesis 2:23 "And Adam said, this is now bone of my bones and flesh of my flesh. She shall be called Woman because she was taken out of man."*

Revelation

- What did Adam say to his wife, and why did he use this phrase?
- Did the wife have to ask a question to get this response?
- To the wife, how would you feel if your husband expressed his feelings like this?

Responsibilities

- Husband, verbally re-affirm your commitment to your wife.

Reverence (hold hands)

- Pray this prayer together: "Father draw us closer side by side in our marriage. We refuse to allow anything or anyone to come between us. Allow us to be inseparable. In Jesus' name, amen."

Date completed:

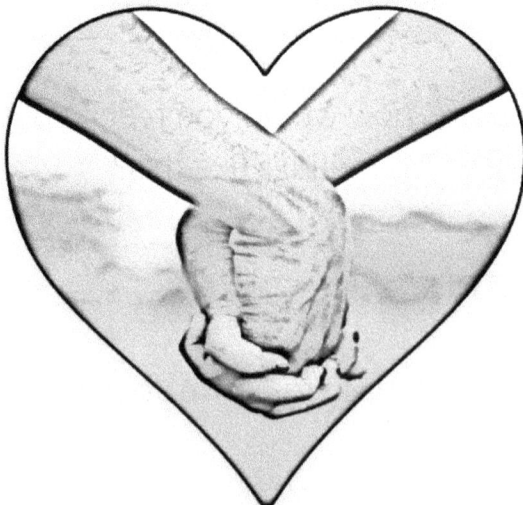

Day 5

Read

♦ *Genesis 2:18 "And Jehovah God said, it is not good that the man should be alone. I will make a helper suitable for him."*

Revelation

♦ Who realized that the man did not need to be alone?

♦ What did God create for the man?

♦ Did God complete the man with his wife or just compliment him with his wife?

Responsibilities

♦ Discuss how you both complement each other.

REVERENCE (HOLD HANDS)

◆ Pray this prayer together: "Father, keep us in re-
membrance that we are complementing each
other in our marriage. We are on the same team.
We celebrate the good times together and hold
each other tight when we go through the tough
times. In Jesus' name, amen."

DATE COMPLETED:

DAY 6

READ

- *Genesis 2:19 "And out of the ground, Jehovah God formed every animal of the field and every fowl of the air, and brought them to Adam to see what he would call them. And whatever Adam called each living creature, that was its name."*

- *Genesis 2:20 "And Adam gave names to all the cattle, and to the birds of the air, and to every animal of the field. But there was not found a suitable helper for Adam."*

REVELATION

- What is God doing in these verses?

- What instruction did He give Adam?

- What did Adam realize after he completed the assignment?

RESPONSIBILITIES

♦ Husband, please share the reasons why your wife is so vital in your life. (Wife, please write them down as he shares.)

REVERENCE (HOLD HANDS)

♦ Pray this prayer together: "Father, please help us to realize that we need each other. Let us make sure that we do not take each other for granted. Let us stay faithful and loyal to each other. In Jesus' name, amen."

DATE COMPLETED:
_____

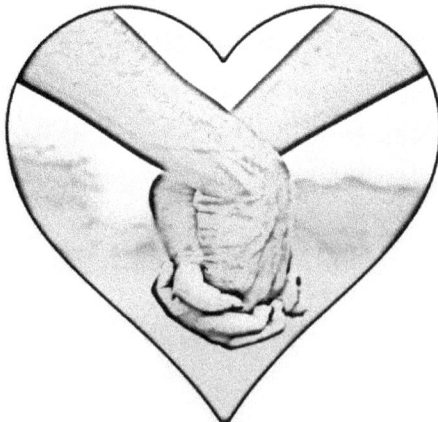

DAY 7

READ

- *Genesis 2:21 "And Jehovah God caused a deep sleep to fall on Adam, and he slept. And He took one of his ribs and closed up the flesh underneath."*

- *Genesis 2:22 "And Jehovah God made the rib (which He had taken from the man) into a woman. And He brought her to the man."*

REVELATION

- Explain what God did to Adam?

- What did He take out of Adam?

- After God created the woman, where did He take her?

- Men, if God took a rib from the side of Adam to create your wife, where should you keep her?

Responsibilities

♦ Men, ask your wife to stand beside you. Let her know how important it is for her to be beside you.

Reverence (hold hands)

♦ Pray his prayer together: "Father, I pray that we will be side by side through anything. Help us to remember that we are a powerful team. In Jesus' name, amen."

Date completed:

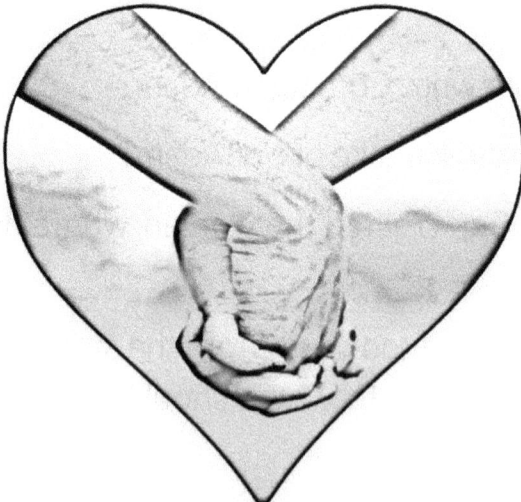

Day 8

Read

- *Isaiah 32:18, "And my people shall dwell in a peaceable home, and in secure dwellings and quiet resting places."*

Revelation

- What are the characteristics of this home?

- How would this atmosphere affect your marriage?

Responsibilities

- Read this verse aloud in every room in your home.

- Type this verse, print, and frame it.

Reverence (hold hands)

- Pray this prayer together: "Father, we agree that this is the atmosphere we want in our home. Our home is free from tension, fear, disorder, abuse, bitterness, and chaos. Our home is filled with love, laughter, and life. In Jesus' name, amen."

Date completed:

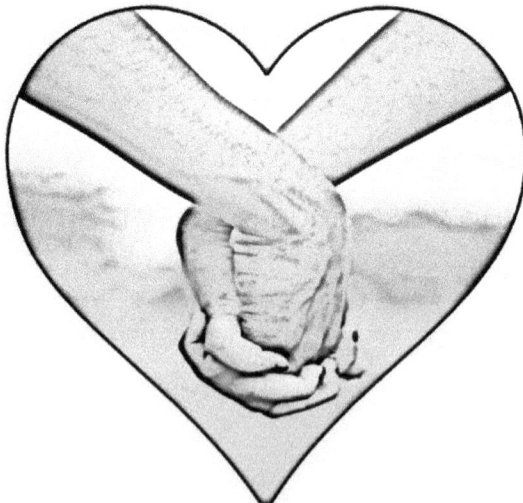

Day 9

Read

- *Ephesians 5:22 "Wives, submit to your own husbands, as to the Lord."*

Revelation

- Wives, to whom should you submit as to the Lord?

- Submission is divided into two syllables:
    - "Sub," means to support
    - "Mission," means plan or direction
    - If the wife is going to support the plan, whose responsibility is it to initiate the mission?

Responsibilities

♦ Designate a time to discuss some descriptive words or phrases that you want your marriage to become. (i.e., peaceful, harmony, inseparable)

Reverence (Hold hands)

♦ Pray this prayer together: "Father, give us a clear picture of submission. Let us know that it is not being controlled, or a doormat, but it is responding to good leadership. Help us to work together to create an atmosphere in our marriage where submission is welcomed and honored. In Jesus' name, amen."

Date completed:

Day 10

Read

- *Ephesians 5:25 "Husbands, love your wives, as Christ loved the church and gave himself up for her."*

Revelation

- What is the responsibility of the husband?

- To whom is this verse comparing the husband?

- In order to love, what must you be willing to do for her?

Responsibilities

- Husbands, place your wife's hand on your heart and let her know she has access to your heart.

REVERENCE (HOLD HANDS)

- ◆ Pray this prayer together: "Father, help us to create godly love in this relationship. Give us the strength to be selfless and learn how to give and receive love from each other. In Jesus' name, amen."

DATE COMPLETED:

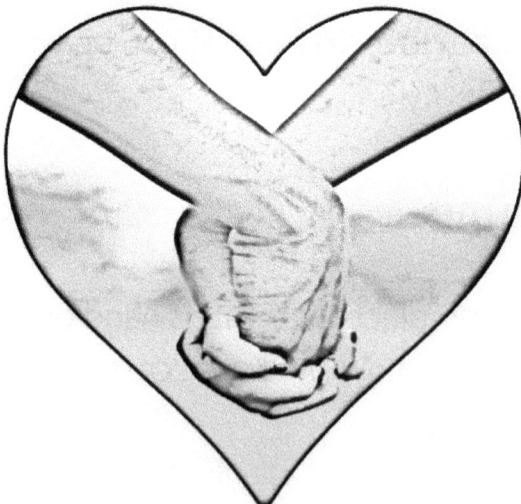

DAY 11

READ

◆ *Ecclesiastes 3:1 "For everything there is a season, and a time for every matter under heaven:"*

REVELATION

◆ How is everything set up?

RESPONSIBILITIES

◆ Discuss your weekly schedule.

◆ Designate some time each week to have a date.

REVERENCE (HOLD HANDS)

♦ Pray this prayer together: "Father, please help us to value and guard our time. Remind us there are 24 hours in one day and we need to manage it. Help us to say "no," to outside negative influences. Let us enjoy the time we have together. In Jesus' name, amen."

DATE COMPLETED:

DAY 12

READ

♦ *Ephesians 4:29 "Let no corrupting talk come out of your mouths, but only such as is good for building up, as fits the occasion, that it may give grace to those who hear."*

REVELATION

♦ What should we refrain from coming out of your mouth?

♦ What is the appropriate communication you should have with each other?

♦ How would this useful communication positively affect your marriage?

Responsibilities

- Share with each other what you value and appreciate in each other.

- Set up some communication boundaries to ensure that your communication does not attack each other

Reverence (Hold hands)

- Pray this prayer together: "Father, we ask you to help us guard our conversation toward each other. Let us be mindful to communicate in a way to build each other up. Let us have open communication and be effective listeners. In Jesus' name, amen."

Date completed:

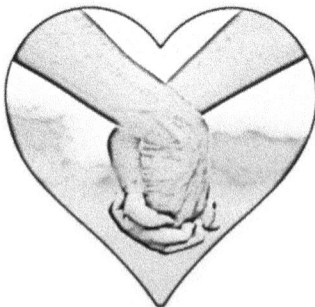

Day 13

Read

- *Proverbs 3:9 "Honor the LORD with your wealth and the first part of your harvest."*

- *Proverbs 3:10 "Then your barns will be full of grain, and your barrels will be overflowing with wine."*

Revelation

- Describe how to manage your finances.
- What will be the benefit?

Responsibilities

- Create a budget.

REVERENCE (HOLD HANDS)

- ◆ Pray this prayer together: "Father, we come into agreement that our finances belong to you, and we are here to steward it. We will work together to manage our finances accordingly. We will be wise in spending and not impulsive. In Jesus' name, amen."

DATE COMPLETED:

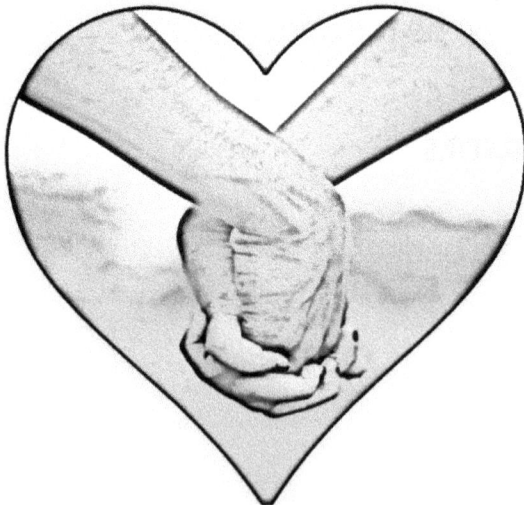

DAY 14

READ

- *Deuteronomy 6:5 "You must love the LORD your God with all your heart, with all your soul, and with all your strength."*

- *Deuteronomy 6:6 "Always remember these commands that I give you today."*

- *Deuteronomy 6:7 "Be sure to teach them to your children. Talk about these commands when you sit in your house and when you walk on the road. Talk about them when you lie down and when you get up."*

REVELATION

- How should you love the Lord?
- To whom should we teach these commands?
- Where should you teach your children?

RESPONSIBILITIES

- ◆ Read these verses to your children.

- ◆ Explain to them that you both love God with all your heart, soul, and strength, and you also love each other the same way.

REVERENCE (HOLD HANDS)

- ◆ Pray this prayer together: "Father, we thank you for blessing us with our children. Help us to love them, teach them, and guide them to love you and to know you as their personal Savior. In Jesus' name, amen."

DATE COMPLETED:

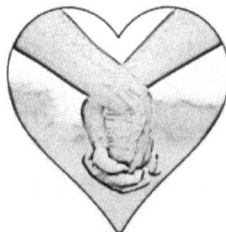

Day 15

Read

- *Proverbs 15:22 "Without counsel plans fail, but with many advisers, they succeed."*

Revelation

- What happens when you do not have wise counsel?

- What is the result when you have many advisors around you?

Responsibilities

- Think of one to two couples that can be advisors to you.

- Explain to the advisors your vision, plans, and how you want them to hold you accountable.

Reverence (hold hands)

- Pray this prayer together: "Father, we desperately want to succeed in our marriage and lives. Please direct us to a healthy couple who will be our advisors to assist us to succeed. In Jesus' name, amen."

Date completed:

Day 16

Read

♦ *2 Timothy 1:7 "For God has not given us the spirit of fear, but of power and of love and of a sound mind."*

Revelation

♦ What is it that God has not given you?

♦ What has He given you?

Responsibilities

♦ Discuss some things you are fearful or concerned about.

REVERENCE (HOLD HANDS)

♦ Pray this prayer together: "Father, we agree that you have not given us a spirit of fear, but of power, love, and a sound mind. We receive this in our marriage. We refuse to be led by fear. In Jesus' name, amen."

DATE COMPLETED:

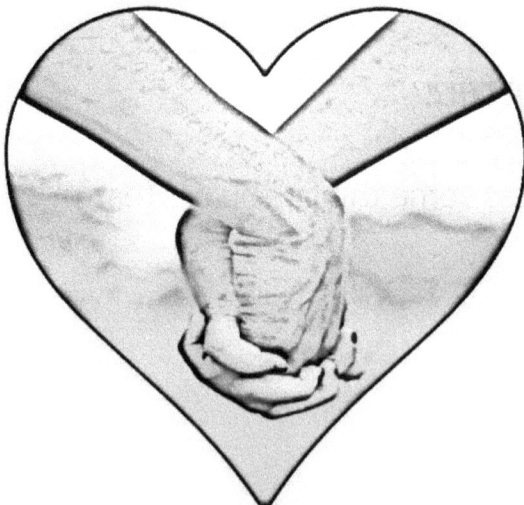

DAY 17

READ

- *Ephesians 4:32 "Be kind to one another, tender-hearted, forgiving one another, as God in Christ forgave you."*

REVELATION

- How should we treat each other?

RESPONSIBILITIES

- Take some time to make sure you have settled any past issues.

REVERENCE (HOLD HANDS)

- Pray this prayer together: "Father, we come into agreement to learn how to treat each other with kindness and respect. Help us to release any wounds and hurts from the past. Help us to view each other in a new light and not from our past. In Jesus' name, amen."

DATE COMPLETED:

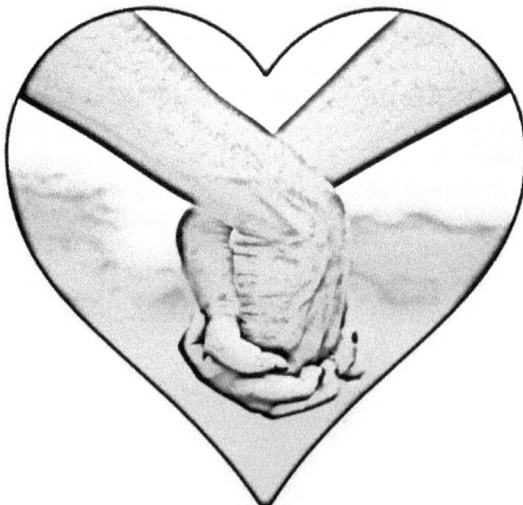

Day 18

Read

♦ *Job 8:21 "He will yet fill your mouth with laughter, and your lips with shouting."*

Revelation

♦ With what will God fill us?

♦ Why is laughter so important to our marriage?

Responsibilities

♦ Do something that will create laughter; watch a comedy movie.

Reverence (hold hands)

- Pray this prayer together: "Father, we want our home and marriage to be filled with laughter. Help us create laughter into our marriage. In Jesus' name, amen."

Date completed:
_____

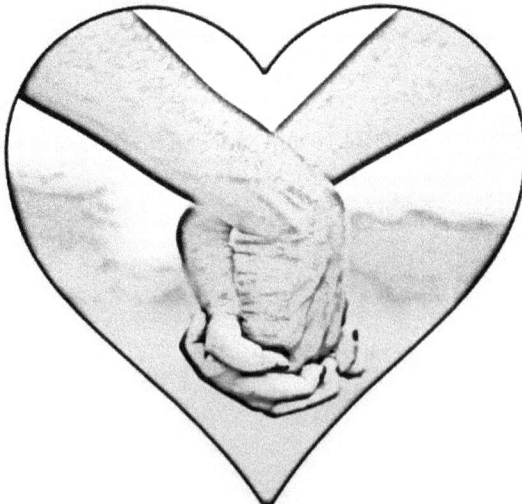

Day 19

Read

- *Psalms 9:1, "I will give thanks to the LORD with all my heart, I will declare all your wonderful deeds."*

Revelation

- What will you offer the Lord?

- What will you declare?

Responsibilities

- Please list why you are thankful.

    1.

    2.

    3.

    4

5.

6.

7.

8.

9.

10.

REVERENCE (HOLD HANDS)

♦ Pray this prayer together: "Father, please teach us
to be more grateful. Help us to see how we are
blessed. Please forgive us for taking each other
for granted and complaining. In Jesus' name,
amen."

DATE COMPLETED:

DAY 20

READ

- *Proverbs 16:3, "Commit your work to the LORD, and your plans will be established."*

REVELATION

- What do we need to commit to the Lord?

- What are the results of committing our plans to the Lord?

RESPONSIBILITIES

- Create goals for:
- 1 month
- 6 months
- 12 months

REVERENCE (HOLD HANDS)

◆ Pray this prayer together: "Father, we commit our marriage and our plans to you. Guide us as we move toward the future. In Jesus' name, amen."

DATE COMPLETED:

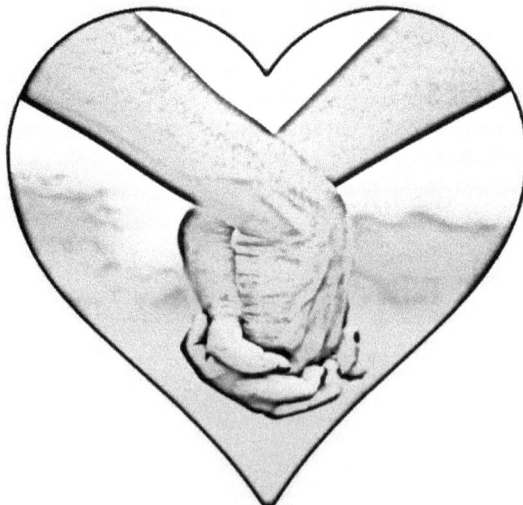

Day 21

READ

- *Isaiah 43:18, "So don't remember what happened in earlier times. Don't think about what happened a long time ago,"*

- *Isaiah 43:19, "Because I am doing something new! Now you will grow like a new plant. Surely you know this is true. I will even make a road in the desert, and rivers will flow through that dry land."*

REVELATION

- What should we eventually do with our past?
- What do we need to focus on?

RESPONSIBILITIES

- ♦ Get a 3x5 card and write down the words: "Our Past."

- ♦ Come into agreement to release it. Rip the card into two.

- ♦ Get another 3x5 card and write down the words: "Our Future" and discuss four dreams you believe to see in your marriage.

REVERENCE (HOLD HANDS)

- ♦ Pray this prayer together: "Father, we agree that we are ready to release the past and embrace our future. Give us the strength to bury our past and not go back and dig it up. We decide today to take the first step toward our future. In Jesus' name, amen."

DATE COMPLETED:

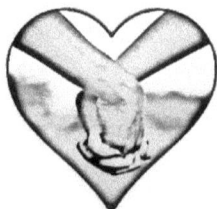

Day 22

READ

- *Song of Solomon 8:3 "His left hand is under my head, and his right hand embraces me!"*

REVELATION

- How is he holding his bride?

- How does a bride feel to be held this way?

RESPONSIBILITIES

- Create some time to hold each other and enjoy each other's presence

REVERENCE (HOLD HANDS)

- Pray this prayer together: "Father, give us a revelation of true intimacy. Help to see, intimacy is more than a physical act, but an emotional bonding. Let our intimacy be pure, meaningful, and passionate. In Jesus' name, amen."

DATE COMPLETED:

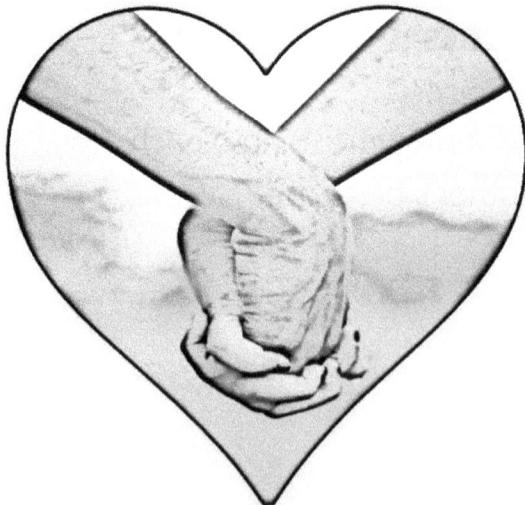

Day 23

Read

- *Proverbs 31:10 "An excellent wife who can find? She is far more precious than jewels."*

- *Proverbs 31:11 "The heart of her husband trusts in her, and he will have no lack of gain."*

- *Pro 31:12 "She does him good, and not harm, all the days of her life."*

Revelation

- What is the value of an excellent wife?
- Where is the heart of her husband?
- How does she treat her husband?

RESPONSIBILITIES

- Men, share with your wife why this is so important to you.

REVERENCE (HOLD HANDS)

- Pray this prayer together: "Father, please give us a revelation of this verse in our marriage. (Wife's prayer): please help me to become a virtuous woman to my husband. Let him trust me with everything. (Husband's prayer) please help me Lord to receive and honor my virtuous wife. Let me treat her like a queen. We ask all of this In Jesus' name, amen."

DATE COMPLETED:

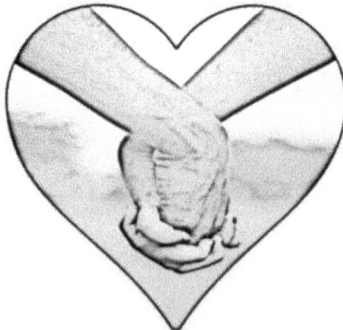

Day 24

Read

- *1Peter 3:7 "Likewise, husbands, live with your wives in an understanding way, showing honor to the woman as the weaker vessel, since they are heirs with you of the grace of life, so that your prayers may not be hindered."*

Revelation

- Husband, how should you love your bride?
- What is the consequence of not treating her the right way?

Responsibilities

- Husband, explain to your bride the qualities that you honor in her.

REVERENCE (HOLD HANDS)

♦ Pray this prayer together: (Prayed by the husband) "Father, help me to treat my bride with respect and honor. Give me ideas how to honor her. In Jesus' name, amen."

DATE COMPLETED:

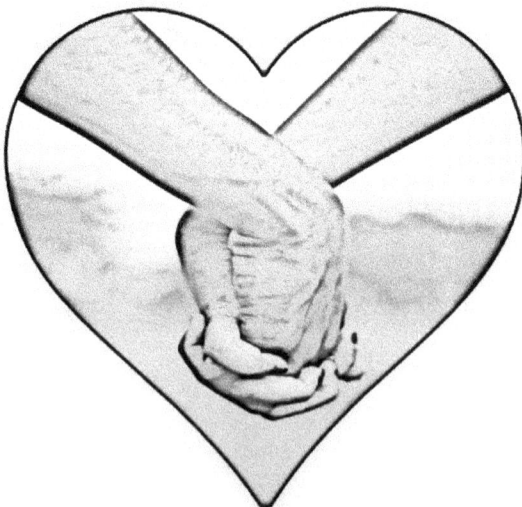

Day 25

Read

♦ *Romans 8:37 "No, in all these things we are more than conquerors through him who loved us."*

Revelation

♦ In how many things are we more than conquerors?

♦ How does God feel about us?

Responsibilities

♦ Make a list of how God has brought you out of difficult experiences.

Reverence (hold hands)

- Pray this prayer together: "Father, we understand that we are more than conquerors in all things. Remind us of this when we are facing difficult situations. May we always know that as a couple, we can face anything.
  In Jesus' name, amen."

Date completed:

Day 26

- *1Co 13:4 "Love is patient and kind; love does not envy or boast; it is not arrogant."*

- *1Co 13:5 "or rude. It does not insist on its own way; it is not irritable or resentful;"*

- *1Co 13:6 "it does not rejoice at wrongdoing, but rejoices with the truth."*

- *1Co 13:7 "Love bears all things, believes all things, hopes all things, endures all things."*

- *1Co 13:8 "Love never ends. As for prophecies, they will pass away; as for tongues, they will cease; as for knowledge, it will pass away."*

REVELATION

- What are the characteristics of love?

- Responsibilities

- Make a list of the characteristics of love and use it as your standard for loving each other.

REVERENCE (HOLD HANDS)

- Pray this prayer together: "Father, teach us to love each other this way. Help us to prefer each other. We want our love to be strong and long-lasting. In Jesus' name, amen."

DATE COMPLETED:

Day 27

Read

- *Colossians 3:23 "Whatever you do, work heartily, as for the Lord and not for men,"*

- *Colossians 3:24 "Knowing that from the Lord you will receive the inheritance as your reward. You are serving the Lord Christ."*

Revelation

- What should be our work ethic?

- What is the result of this work ethic?

Responsibilities

- Adjust your work ethic toward your employment or your business.

Reverence (hold hands)

♦ Pray this prayer together: "Father, we agree that we have a strong work ethic. We commit to put our all into our marriage and our employment opportunities. In Jesus' name, amen."

Date completed:

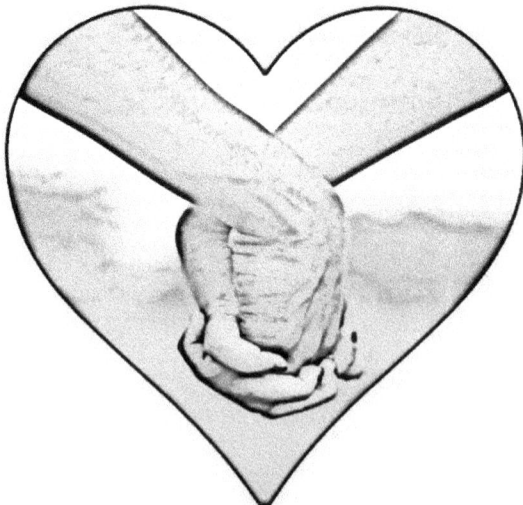

Day 28

Read

♦ *Isaiah 54:17 "No weapon that is formed against thee shall prosper; and every tongue that shall rise against thee in judgment thou shalt condemn. This is the heritage of the servants of Jehovah, and their righteousness which is of me, saith Jehovah."*

Revelation

♦ What is the result if something is formed against you?

Responsibilities

♦ Make a list of outside hindrances that are affecting your marriage.

Reverence (hold hands)

- Pray this prayer together: "Father, we agree that we have a covenant with you. Help us not to take revenge if we have been wronged by others. Let us stay focused on our marriage and stay productive. In Jesus' name, amen."

Date completed:

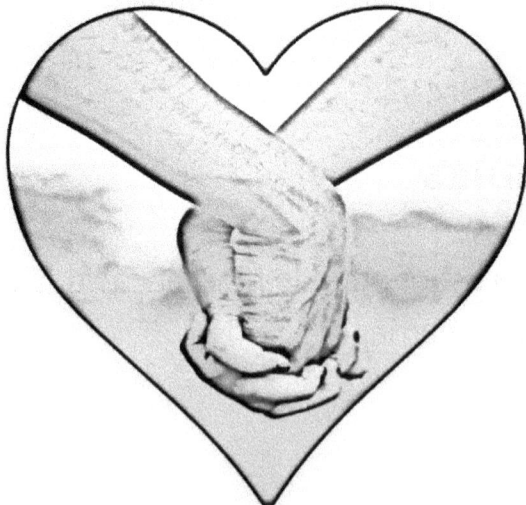

Day 29

Read

- *Proverbs 3:27 "Do everything you possibly can for those who need help."*

Revelation

- What should we do, whenever possible?

Responsibilities

- Look for a way to help someone else this week.

REVERENCE (HOLD HANDS)

- ♦ Pray this prayer together: "Father, remind us that we are blessed. Show us opportunities that we can be a blessing to others. In Jesus' name, amen.

DATE COMPLETED: _____

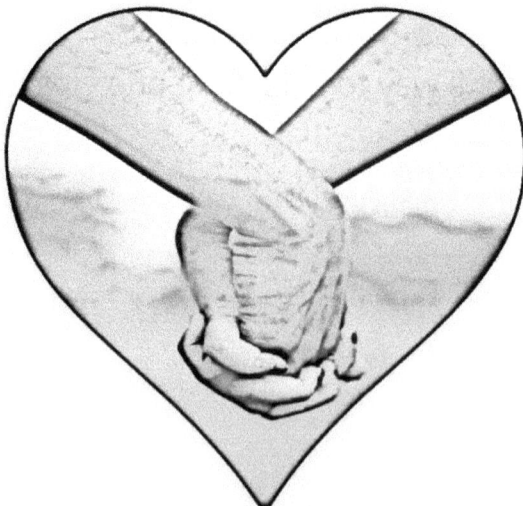

Day 30

Read

♦ *Galatians 6:9 "And let us not grow weary of doing good, for in due season we will reap, if we do not give up."*

Revelation

♦ What should we do when things are going well?

♦ What is the result of not growing weary?

Responsibilities

♦ Make a list of what you are doing that is keeping your marriage in the ONENESS state.

REVERENCE (HOLD HANDS)

♦ Pray this prayer together: "Father, we agree that we have come a long way. We refuse to let anything stop our progress. We will not let an isolated incident cause us to stop our progress. Let us enjoy our due season of oneness. In Jesus' name, amen."

DATE COMPLETED:

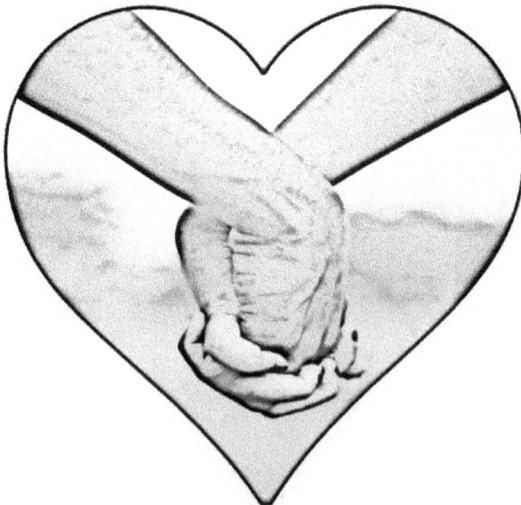

Connect with David Banks, PhD

I would love to come to your country, city, church, group, or organization to speak, train or consult and conduct a Virtual Marriage Retreat

Schedule David Banks, Ph.D. as a Speaker/Trainer For:

Marriage

Family

Leadership Development

Purpose Discovery

Discovering Your Original Design

Virtual Training

Success

Motivation

David Banks, PhD

Phone: 423-508-9642

Email: Noblemarriages@gmail.com

@dbmarriagecoach

LinkedIn - davidbanksphd

Facebook - https://www.facebook.com/groups/NobleSuccessGroup/

www.ingramcontent.com/pod-product-compliance
Lightning Source LLC
Chambersburg PA
CBHW071429040426
42445CB00012BA/1308